Victoria Justice

ABDO
Publishing Company

Big
Buddy BOOKS
Buddy Bios

by Sarah Tieck

VISIT US AT
www.abdopublishing.com

Published by ABDO Publishing Company, PO Box 398166, Minneapolis, Minnesota 55439.

Printed in the United States of America, North Mankato, Minnesota.
102012
112013

 PRINTED ON RECYCLED PAPER

Coordinating Series Editor: Rochelle Baltzer
Contributing Editors: Stephanie Hedlund, Marcia Zappa
Graphic Design: Maria Hosley
Cover Photograph: *AP Photo*: John Shearer/Invision for MTV.com.
Interior Photographs/Illustrations: *AP Photo*: Rex Features via AP Images (p. 19), PRNewsFoto/Nickelodeon, Lisa Rose (p. 15), PRNewsFoto/Nickelodeon, Lisa Rose/Nickelodeon (p. 13), John Shearer/Invision for MTV.com (p. 24), Charles Sykes (p. 25), Donald Traill (p. 27); *Getty Images*: Michael Buckner/WireImage (p. 17), Gregg DeGuire/WireImage (p. 11), Charley Gallay/WireImage (pp. 13, 19, 23), Jesse Grant/WireImage (p. 9), Jon Kopaloff/FilmMagic (p. 5), George Pimentel (p. 21), Christopher Polk/KCA2011/Getty Images for Nickelodeon (p. 29), Theo Wargo/Staff/WireImage for Turner (p. 7); *iStockphoto*: ©iStockphoto.com/photoquest7 (p. 9).

Cataloging-in-Publication Data

Tieck, Sarah.
  Victoria Justice: famous actress & singer / Sarah Tieck.
    p. cm. -- (Big buddy biographies)
  ISBN 978-1-61783-750-0
  1. Justice, Victoria, 1993- --Juvenile literature. 2. Teenage actors--United States--Biography--Juvenile literature. 3. Television actors and actresses--United States--Biography--Juvenile literature. I. Title.
  791.4502/8092--dc22
  [B]
                        2012946486

Victoria Justice

Contents

Rising Star

Victoria Justice is an actress and a singer. She has appeared in television shows and movies. She is best known for starring in the television show *Victorious*. She has also released popular music.

Victoria plays Tori Vega on *Victorious.*

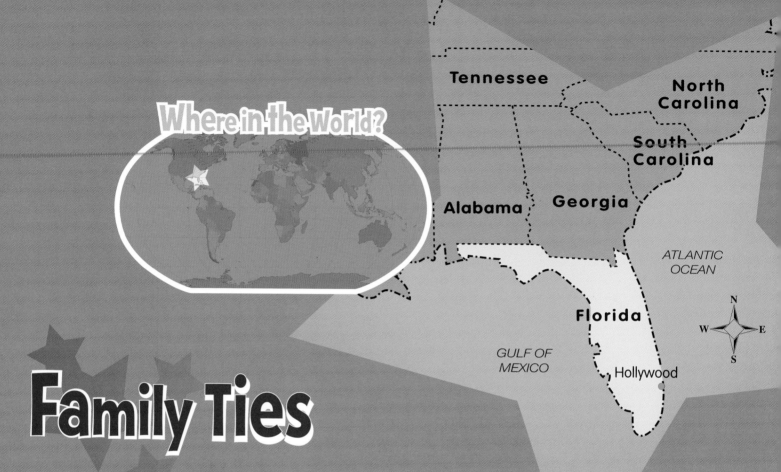

Where in the World?

Tennessee

North Carolina

South Carolina

Alabama

Georgia

ATLANTIC OCEAN

Florida

GULF OF MEXICO

Hollywood

N
W   E
S

Family Ties

Victoria Dawn Justice was born in Hollywood, Florida, on February 19, 1993. Her parents are Serene Justice-Reed and Zack Justice. Her stepfather is Mark Reed. She has a younger half sister named Madison.

Victoria's family is Puerto Rican, English, German, and Irish. Victoria values her background.

6

Victoria's family is very proud of her success. Sometimes Serene attends events with her.

Starting Out

Victoria became interested in acting when she was just eight. After watching a **commercial**, she knew she wanted to be an actress. So, she tried out for **professional** acting parts. She was in several commercials.

When Victoria was about ten, her family moved to California. There, she got more acting work. In 2003, she appeared on a popular television show called *Gilmore Girls*.

Victoria worked hard to gain experience and get parts.

California is home to many actors and actresses. A lot of movies and television shows are made there.

HOLLYWOOD

A Young Actress

Over the next few years, Victoria had many different parts. Most of them were small. But, they helped her grow as an actress.

In 2005, Victoria acted in a short movie called *Mary*. Also that year, she got a main **role** on the Nickelodeon show *Zoey 101*. In 2006, Victoria got a part in the movie *The Garden*.

Victoria played the character Lola Martinez on *Zoey 101*. Jamie Lynn Spears (*right*) starred on the show as Zoey Brooks.

Lights! Camera! Action!

Victoria kept appearing in small parts on Nickelodeon shows. In 2009, she was on *The Naked Brothers Band*, *iCarly*, and *True Jackson, VP*. Also that year, she appeared in a popular television movie called *Spectacular!*

Victoria played a fighter named Shelby Marx on *iCarly*.

Victoria starred in *Spectacular!* with Tammin Sursok, Simon Curtis, and Nolan Gerard Funk (*left to right*).

Zoey 101 ended in 2008. But, the show's producer said he wanted to work with Victoria again. He had seen that she could sing, dance, and act. So, he created the show *Victorious* just for her.

Victorious often features singing and dancing.

KARAOKE DOKIE

Big Break

In 2010, Victoria began starring in *Victorious*. This was an important step in her acting **career**. On the show, Victoria plays Tori Vega. Tori is a girl who attends a **performing** arts high school. She wants to be a singer. Soon, *Victorious* became one of Nickelodeon's most popular shows!

Pop Star

Aside from being an actress, Victoria is a talented singer. In 2010, she recorded "Make It Shine." This song plays at the start of *Victorious*.

Victoria's music is featured on albums from her **role** on *Victorious*. Her popular songs include "Freak the Freak Out" and "Beggin' on Your Knees."

In 2011, Victoria teamed up with Miranda Cosgrove and other *Victorious* and *iCarly* actors. They sang a song called "Leave It All to Shine."

Victoria sings and helps write songs.

New Opportunities

More people noticed Victoria's talent. Soon, she had more chances to act in movies. In 2012, Victoria appeared in a movie called *The First Time*.

Then, Victoria got a starring **role** in a **comedy** called *Fun Size*. She was chosen over many other actresses for the part. The movie came out in fall 2012.

Victoria worked with Dylan O'Brien, Britt Robertson, and Jon Kasdan (*left to right*) in *The First Time*.

In 2011, Victoria and her *Victorious* costars took part in a flash mob. They performed "All I Want Is Everything."

An Actress's Life

As an actress, Victoria is very busy! She must practice **lines** for her **roles**. During filming, she works on a **set** for several hours each day.

As a singer, Victoria also spends time practicing and recording songs. Sometimes she practices **performing** them.

Victoria talks to reporters about her work and fashion.

Victoria's talents as an actress and a singer have made her popular. She has many fans! Victoria appears in magazines. She also talks to reporters for news stories.

In 2010, Victoria was part of the Macy's Thanksgiving Day Parade.

Off the Screen

Victoria is often on set, singing, or traveling for her career. But when she has free time, she spends it with friends and family. She likes watching movies, swimming, ice skating, and shopping.

Victoria also likes to work with groups that help people in need. Sometimes, she attends events to raise money for certain causes.

In 2010, Victoria helped with Girl Up. Girl Up supports education and health care for girls around the world.

Buzz

Victoria's opportunities continue to grow. In 2012, she worked on the third and final season of *Victorious*. She also recorded more songs. And, she looks forward to acting in more movies.

Fans are excited to see what's next for Victoria Justice. Many believe she has a bright **future**!

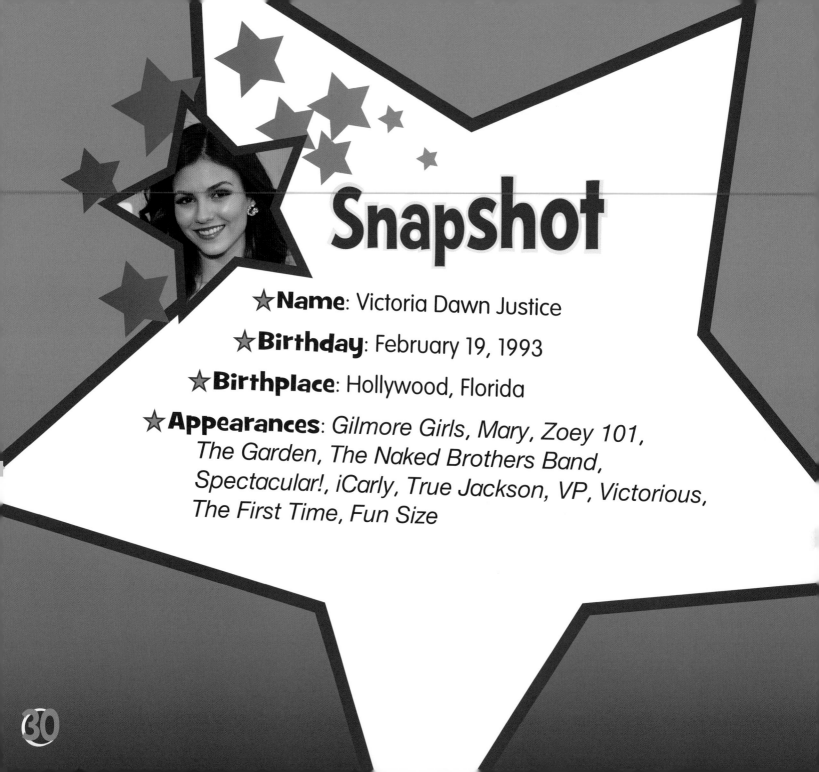

Snapshot

★**Name**: Victoria Dawn Justice

★**Birthday**: February 19, 1993

★**Birthplace**: Hollywood, Florida

★**Appearances**: Gilmore Girls, Mary, Zoey 101, The Garden, The Naked Brothers Band, Spectacular!, iCarly, True Jackson, VP, Victorious, The First Time, Fun Size

Important Words

career work a person does to earn money for living.

comedy a funny story.

commercial (kuh-MUHR-shuhl) a short message on television or radio that helps sell a product.

future (FYOO-chuhr) a time that has not yet occurred.

lines the words an actor says in a play, a movie, or a show.

perform to do something in front of an audience.

producer a person who oversees the making of a movie, a play, an album, or a radio or television show.

professional (pruh-FEHSH-nuhl) working for money rather than for pleasure.

release to make available to the public.

role a part an actor plays.

set the place where a movie or a television show is recorded.

Web Sites

To learn more about Victoria Justice, visit ABDO Publishing Company online. Web sites about Victoria Justice are featured on our Book Links page. These links are routinely monitored and updated to provide the most current information available.

www.abdopublishing.com

Index

DATE DUE